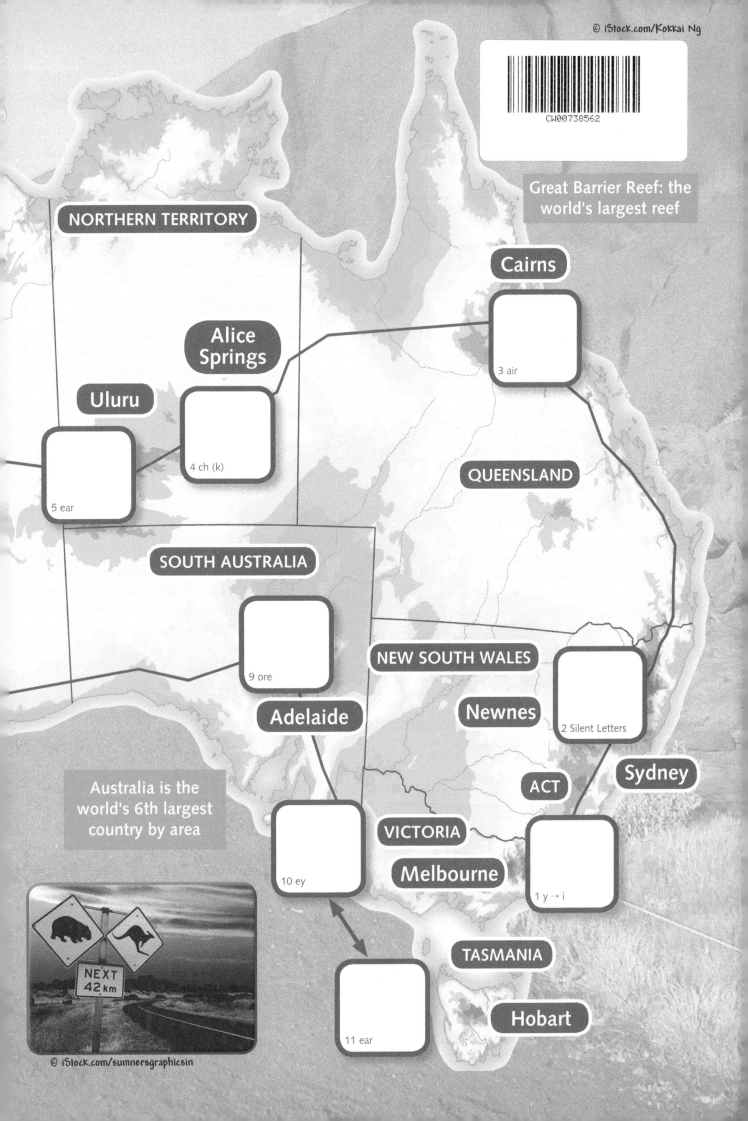

© iStock.com/Kokkai Ng

CW00738562

Great Barrier Reef: the world's largest reef

NORTHERN TERRITORY

Cairns

3 air

Alice Springs

4 ch (k)

Uluru

5 ear

QUEENSLAND

SOUTH AUSTRALIA

9 ore

NEW SOUTH WALES

Newnes

2 Silent Letters

Adelaide

Sydney

ACT

Australia is the world's 6th largest country by area

VICTORIA

Melbourne

10 ey

1 y → i

NEXT 42 km

© iStock.com/sumnersgraphicsin

TASMANIA

Hobart

11 ear

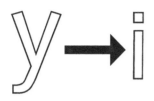

Happiness

By Sophie

Read the words.

Remember plurals! Set 1 (16 words)	Adding ness/less/ful Set 2 (18 words)	Adding er/est Set 3 (18 words)	Adding ly/ment Set 4 (18 words)
flies	tidiness	easier	cheekily
cries	liveliness	merrier	merrily
spies	cosiness	cheekier	cheerily
ladies	oiliness	healthier	prettily
armies	penniless	sleepier	luckily
cities	happiness	happier	angrily
puppies	business	fruitier	happily
bullies	beautiful	lazier	busily
studies	plentiful	earlier	funnily
ponies	fanciful	hilliest	easily
parties	dutiful	silkiest	heavily
stories	pitiful	ugliest	clumsily
countries	merciful	prettiest	gloomily
pennies	readiness	curliest	stealthily
families	dizziness	nastiest	hungrily
enemies	loneliness	easiest	temporarily
16 words so far	emptiness	busiest	necessarily
	pitiless	greediest	merriment
	34 words so far	52 words so far	70 words so far

One Minute Wonders

	up to 39 Sparking	40–49 Glowing	50–59 Burning	60–69 Sizzling	70+ Red hot!
Score/Date					
Score/Date					

4

Read the poem then draw the picture.

Happiness!

Tidiness means everything in place
Liveliness is wanting to race
Cosiness, a big comfy chair

Oiliness, a problem with hair
Penniless might mean nothing to lend
But happiness is having a good friend!

Practise writing.

Build your word power.

Brilliant! You are off!

Luckily, all your training has gone to plan; you are ready to start your challenge. You have your Camelback water pack and some energy sweets. Sydney is easily one of the world's most beautiful city marathon courses. Happily, there is a cooling breeze as you run over the famous Harbour Bridge. The samba bands are drumming and the crowds are plentiful near the spectacular Opera House; they cheer you on to stop you flagging. You can feel a blister starting already and will treat it with surgical spirit later. A great first run in a time of just under four hours.

Sneaky Silent Letters

n g k t b

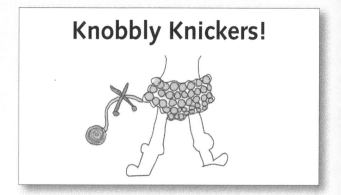

Knobbly Knickers!

By Alex

Read the words.

Solemn Column **Set 1** (12 words)	Design a Sign **Set 2** (17 words)	Knobbly Knickers **Set 3** (20 words)	Hustle and Bustle **Set 4** (20 words)	Numb Thumbs **Set 5** (20 words)
solemn	**design**	knobbly	hustle	numb
column	**sign**	knickers	bustle	thumbs
autumn	gnashing	knock	thistle	**doubt**
hymn	**foreign**	**know**	castle	comb
condemn	reign	knot	whistle	bomb
condemned	gnaw	knight	**listen**	tomb
columns	gnat	knob	often	climb
solemnly	gnome	knit	fasten	crumb
government	gnawed	knife	soften	dumb
governments	gnarled	kneel	glisten	debt
condemning	reigned	knack	rustle	jamb
governmental	champagne	knead	bristle	lamb
12 words so far	signpost	knew	trestle	limb
	gnawing	knee	nestle	womb
	campaign	knitwear	jostle	climbed
	foreigner	knighthood	wrestle	succumbed
	campaigning	kneeling	moisten	doubtless
	29 words so far	knowledge	mortgage	plumber
		knuckle	whistling	bombing
		knitted	apostle	indebted
		49 words so far	69 words so far	89 words so far

One Minute Wonders

	up to 39 Sparking	40–49 Glowing	50–59 Burning	60–69 Sizzling	70+ Red hot!
Score/Date					
Score/Date					

6

Read the story then draw the picture.

Needing to design a new sign for my autumn collection of knobbly knickers, I took a boat to Thistle Island. What a hustle and bustle there was at the port! I arrived safely at Knock Castle Hotel but soon I was so cold that my thumbs became numb. I tried to whistle a happy tune but my teeth kept chattering and gnashing together. Never again!

Practise writing.

Build your word power.

Well done!

ear
ey
ore
eer
ie ei
are
ear
ch (k)
air
Silent Letters
y → i

Brilliant! You made it to the next stage!

After four hours on the bus you reach Newnes for the Glow Worm Marathon. You jostle for position at the start, so you can begin at a good pace. Trying to leap a creek, you splash in and run along an old mine cutting with squelching feet! Later, you nearly twist your ankle on a gnarled piece of wood. After emerging from the humid rainforest, you see a sign to the tunnel. Inside, the sight of millions of glow worms is magical. You finish ahead of many others in a time of 3 hours 48 minutes. A cold bath is needed to relieve your aching muscles.

Hairy Pair

By Georgia

Read the words.

Set 1 (11 words)	Set 2 (20 words)	Set 3 (20 words)	Set 4 (20 words)
hairy	**air**	fairies	upstairs
pair	stair	dairies	fairness
despair	chair	airer	airless
repaired	laird	armchair	fairly
unfair	fairs	airy	airline
funfair	flair	airing	impair
Blair	airs	staircase	disrepair
fair	pairs	downstairs	clairvoyant
dairy	hair	pushchair	hairdresser
eclairs	lair	wheelchair	hairiest
Alistair	lairs	hairstyle	despairing
11 words so far	paired	chairing	repairing
	aired	affair	airily
	cairn	fairground	hairier
	fairer	fairy	unfairly
	airport	haircut	haircutting
	repair	hairband	staircases
	despaired	highchair	chairperson
	airfare	chairlift	hairstyling
	hairless	fairgrounds	unrepairable
	31 words so far	51 words so far	71 words so far

One Minute Wonders

	up to 39 Sparking	40–49 Glowing	50–59 Burning	60–69 Sizzling	70+ Red hot!
Score/Date					
Score/Date					

8

Read the story then draw the picture.

[blank framed box for drawing]

The hairy pair were in despair! With a mighty crash, they had smashed their brand new bikes and had to carry them off to be repaired.

"It's so unfair! Now we will be too late for the funfair!" groaned Blair.

"I know! Forget the fair. We will go to the dairy for some cream and make some chocolate eclairs!" announced Alistair.

Practise writing.

[blank lined writing area]

Build your word power.

[blank box]

Well done!
ear
ey
ore
eer
ie ei
are
ear
ch (k)
air
Silent Letters
y → i

Brilliant! You made it to the next stage!

3

Your 80-hour bus journey to Cairns is gruelling and airless. You've little time to recover before tackling the next 42 kilometres. Before the start, you tuck your snake-bite kit into your backpack and hope you will not need it. After an hour, your legs feel as if you are running upstairs! The loud and quite electrifying sound of a green catbird and a pair of electric blue ulysses butterflies lifts your spirits. It's exciting that possums and tree-climbing kangaroos could be watching you! As you feel mentally exhausted, you are happy just to finish.

ch (k)

Chaos in the Chemist

by Jenny

Read the words.

Set 1 (10 words)	Set 2 (18 words)	Set 3 (18 words)	Set 4 (18 words)
Christmas	**character**	schooner	charisma
chronic	chord	headache	scholastic
stomach	chrome	schooling	scholarship
ache	scheme	anchors	archangel
chaos	ached	toothache	orchestral
chemist	monarch	Christian	mechanical
school	echo	technical	melancholy
choir	anchor	bronchitis	schizophrenic
chorus	orchid	chaotic	chrysanthemum
echoed	chlorine	architect	technology
10 words so far	archive	monarchy	chameleon
	achy	mechanic	architecture
	epoch	orchestra	chlorinated
	scholar	chemical	chaotically
	chasm	synchronise	characteristic
	ochre	cholera	archaeology
	aching	chlorophyll	chronological
	technique	chemistry	archaeological
	28 words so far	46 words so far	64 words so far

	up to 39 Sparking	40–49 Glowing	50–59 Burning	60–69 Sizzling	70+ Red hot!
Score/Date					
Score/Date					

Read the story then draw the picture.

Just before Christmas, I had a chronic stomach ache and needed some medicine. But there was chaos in the chemist because a school choir was singing a loud chorus out of tune. It echoed all around, making people mad!

Practise writing.

Build your word power.

Well done!

ear
ey
ore
eer
ie ei
are
ear
ch (k)
air
Silent Letters
y → i

Brilliant! You made it to the next stage!

4

Thirty-five hours by bus to Alice Springs and you arrive hot and sticky with a chronic headache. It is difficult to think about running. However, the next day, you're excited to start in the dark at 6am in freezing conditions and head straight out into the arid desert. You watch the sun come up on the bronze escarpments of the MacDonnell mountain range; the scenery is stunning. After three hours, you have a second wind and feel strong again. Your finisher's medal is made of a piece of red centre rock!

Read the syllables.

Six syllable types

Closed	elp	ulf	ank	ost	imp	ult	and	uct	olt	empt
Open	gra	pre	pri	mo	gla	zy	re	ho	hu	la
Evil e	ele	one	ume	ine	ade	eme	ise	age	ule	ope
Vowel	bai	way	fee	rea	goa	low	goo	few	cue	lew
-r	chur	lar	irk	snor	urst	ster	smir	bor	snar	ther
-le	-cle	-ble	-fle	-dle	-kle	-gle	-tle	-ple	-sle	-dle

Got it? ☐

***Run Australia* sounds**

walk	chron	cair	umb	cha	air	knot
lair	chor	talk	knock	hair	tech	wri
chem	calm	white	airn	knee	orch	wrin
wrap	dair	sch	climb	mech	comb	bair

Got it? ☐

Prefixes and suffixes

super-	-like	-dom	en-	ex-	-ward	ir-
ambi-	il-	auto-	ante-	extra-	out-	trans-
contra-	-ish	-ability	-hood	-ship	post-	-some

Got it? ☐

Fiery Phrases! 1

Happiness 	**Knobbly Knickers!** 	**Hairy Pair** 	**Chaos in the Chemist** 

Read the phrases.

Set 1	Set 2	Set 3
such beautiful babies	up to your knees	take a chair
all the families	stay calm	two pairs of shoes
so many parties	half and half	at the dairy
his dutiful son	a leaping salmon	it's so unfair
a merciful escape	don't wriggle	off to the airport
he said gloomily	who is it	an airless day
did it clumsily	the wrong way	in a state of disrepair
working away busily	give an answer	go downstairs now
she shouted happily	climb to the top	don't despair
they moved stealthily	rule of thumb	he has real flair
a pitiful excuse	no doubt about it	drop the anchor
the child screamed angrily	comb your hair	go to the chemist
funnily enough	a load of crumbs	it echoed all around
the curliest hair	the rustling leaves	sing the chorus
some fruitier drinks	a difficult campaign	chronic earache
great happiness	tall columns of smoke	what a character
unnecessarily difficult	the wrong signpost	synchronise your watches
they ate hungrily	a long reign	she has charisma
the silkiest coat	soften the butter	time for chemistry
in earlier times	listen to this hymn	it's chaos here
20 phrases	20 phrases	20 phrases

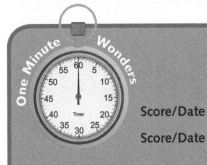

	up to 29 Sparking	30–39 Glowing	40–49 Burning	50–59 Sizzling	60+ Red hot!
Score/Date					
Score/Date					

ear

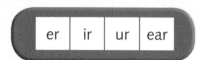

| er | ir | ur | ear |

Read the words.

Set 1 (10 words)	Set 2 (10 words)	Set 3 (11 words)	Set 4 (11 words)
Earl	pearls	yearning	relearn
earn	earns	earning	researcher
research	earls	earthly	researching
early	earned	earldom	rehearsing
search	learnt	unearth	overheard
pearl	yearn	searches	rehearsal
heard	dearth	searchlights	unearthly
earth	hearse	learner	rehearsals
learn	yearned	learning	relearning
rehearse	pearly	earner	unearthing
10 words so far	20 words so far	unearthed	researchable
		31 words so far	42 words so far

One Minute Wonders

	up to 39 Sparking	40–49 Glowing	50–59 Burning	60–69 Sizzling	70+ Red hot!
Score/Date					
Score/Date					

14

Read the story then draw the picture.

The Earl needed to earn some money for his music research. Early one morning, he set off to search for some pearl necklaces that he had heard were hidden in the earth at the bottom of the lake. He wanted to help everyone learn how to rehearse better.

Practise writing.

Build your word power.

Brilliant! You made it to the next stage!

You travel 440 kilometres by bus to Uluru to run the Outback Marathon. You learn that Ayers Rock, a sandstone formation rising 853 metres above sea level, is sacred to the Aboriginal people. It glows red at dawn and sunset. Running is difficult in the heat, especially when the red earth is soft, but luckily it is sometimes hard packed. A flock of grey and pink cockatoos nearby and a wedge-tailed eagle soaring high above take your mind off the blisters that are forming on your feet. This marathon has been exhausting but exhilarating.

Well done!
ear
ey
ore
eer
ie ei
are
ear
ch (k)
air
Silent Letters
y → i

Hare on a Mare

By Jacob

air | are

Read the words.

Set 1 (7 words)	Set 2 (18 words)	Set 3 (18 words)	Set 4 (18 words)	Set 5 (18 words)
hare	**square**	prepared	hare-brained	glassware
mare	**dare**	airfare	hectare	rarefied
share	**declare**	aware	daresay	awareness
Clare	**prepare**	bareback	nightmare	ensnaring
care	**compare**	barebacked	snaring	comparing
stare	glare	barefaced	declared	aftercare
scare	fare	barefoot	ensnare	daredevil
7 words so far	flare	barely	carefree	nightmarish
	rare	beware	flaring	declaring
	snare	careless	flare-up	carefully
	bare	scary	rarer	area
	glares	compared	welfare	unaware
	snared	squarely	sharing	preparing
	cared	threadbare	fieldfare	carelessly
	dared	hardware	scarecrow	caretaker
	careful	daring	warfare	scaremonger
	glaring	harebell	ensnared	warehouses
	rarely	caring	warehouse	over-careful
	25 words so far	*43 words so far*	*61 words so far*	*79 words so far*

One Minute Wonders

	up to 39 Sparking	40–49 Glowing	50–59 Burning	60–69 Sizzling	70+ Red hot!
Score/Date					
Score/Date					

16

Read the limerick then draw the picture.

[blank drawing box]

There once was a hare on a mare
Who had some sweet toffees to share
Though Clare did not care
She soon stopped to stare
Then he shouted and gave her a scare!

Practise writing.

[blank writing lines]

Build your word power.

[blank box]

Brilliant! You made it to the next stage!

Well done!
ear
ey
ore
eer
ie ei
are
ear
ch (k)
air
Silent Letters
y → i

Another massive journey of 40 hours, but you can stare out at this amazing country, spotting kangaroos and wallabies on the way. It is also a chance to prepare yourself mentally for the next run. It's rare for Broome not to have clear blue skies all July and the conditions are perfect as you start at 7am on the firm sand of Cable Beach. Luckily, the beach is open again after two sightings of 3 metre crocodiles the week before! You have a great run and finish in 3 hours 40 minutes. Hurrah!

ie ei

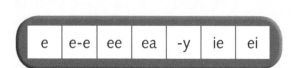

| e | e-e | ee | ea | -y | ie | ei |

Thief in Briefs

By Harry

Read the words.

ie i before e			ei except after c
Set 1 (11 words)	**Set 2** (16 words)	**Set 3** (16 words)	**Set 4** (16 words)
thief	**piece**	briefly	**recieve**
briefs	achieve	diesel	deceive
field	brief	mischief	ceiling
fiend	shriek	fielder	perceive
shrieked	grieve	grieving	conceit
priest	shield	shrieking	deceit
handkerchief	chiefs	disbelief	conceive
niece	siege	achieving	receipt
believe	yield	handkerchiefs	perceived
chief	shrieks	believing	conceited
grief	grieved	mischievous	deceitful
11 words so far	belief	achievable	deceitfully
	fiendish	believable	conceitedly
	achieved	unbelievable	inconceivable
	briefest	unbelievably	seize
	fielded	unachievable	protein
	27 words so far	*43 words so far*	*59 words so far*

One Minute Wonders

	up to 39 Sparking	40–49 Glowing	50–59 Burning	60–69 Sizzling	70+ Red hot!
Score/Date					
Score/Date					

18

Read the story then draw the picture.

The thief in briefs raced out of the field.

"You fiend!" shrieked the priest. "Give me back that handkerchief. It belongs to my niece. Believe me, the chief of police will give you grief!"

Practise writing.

Build your word power.

Brilliant! You made it to the next stage!

7

You complete a 35 hour bus trip to Perth, the capital of Western Australia, which is in one of only five Mediterranean climate zones in the world. You can hardly believe it when there is a storm as you arrive. You hope it will keep the fiendish redback spiders away! You only have time for a brief rest before the Perth to Surf Marathon. A blackened toenail has now come off and you have to keep stretching a calf muscle that is very tight. Having to stop means you have a slower time, but you have at least finished!

eer

Cheering Meerkats

By Lucia

Read the words.

Set 1 (9 words)	Set 2 (14 words)	Set 3 (14 words)	Set 4 (14 words)
meerkat	cheer	meerkats	cheerfully
peered	sneer	cheerful	cheerier
eerie	jeer	veneer	volunteers
sheer	leer	reindeer	auctioneer
mountaineer	peer	sneering	buccaneer
engineer	steer	cheerless	cameleer
cheered	veer	eerily	pioneer
careered	beer	eeriest	engineers
deer	jeered	mountaineers	orienteer
9 words so far	sneered	eerier	engineering
	steers	mutineer	mountaineering
	career	domineer	volunteering
	jeering	volunteer	domineering
	peering	commandeer	orienteering
	23 words so far	37 words so far	51 words so far

One Minute Wonders

	up to 39 Sparking	40–49 Glowing	50–59 Burning	60–69 Sizzling	70+ Red hot!
Score/Date					
Score/Date					

20

Read the story then draw the picture.

Martin the meerkat peered at his mates through the eerie mist at the summit.

"Hooray!" he shouted in sheer delight. "I am now a mountaineer as well as an engineer!"

All his friends cheered noisily as he careered down the hill, scattering the deer in all directions.

Practise writing.

Build your word power.

Brilliant! You made it to the next stage!

Well done!
ear
ey
ore
eer
ie ei
are
ear
ch (k)
air
Silent Letters
y → i

Sheer luxury – a flight to Christmas Island. You give a cheer when you arrive as you are there when the annual red crab mass migration (about 120 million) happens; it is an eerie sight. Your marathon starts at the top of the island, 260 metres above sea level, surrounded by tropical rainforest. Doing one marathon is tough enough, but running several in a row takes its toll. Your knees complain about the hot hard road and you have to push yourself to run through the pain. Volunteers are there to give you a massage at the end!

21

Sizzling Syllables! ②

Read the syllables.

Ski the South Pole review

goy	our	stea	auze	poi	uice	ook
uise	spoi	ool	craw	pow	dir	uit
dau	chow	roy	ouge	ood	trea	thir
wrap	ound	ead	brow	raw	oint	prou

Got it? ☐

New *Run Australia* patterns

mare	prie	ceit	care	ieve	ief	ceil
cei	earch	ield	ceive	teer	snare	earth
earl	leer	iend	ware	sei	cheer	flare
pare	chie	tein	neer	iece	fare	fien

Got it? ☐

All *Run Australia* so far

calf	fair	synch	earn	ief	know	dare
chlor	ield	wrap	meer	ceit	clair	iece
knit	jeer	rhyme	pair	half	lear	chas
ceil	doubt	stair	ieve	glare	chol	reer

Got it? ☐

22

Fiery Phrases! ②

Search for Pearls	Hare on a Mare	Thief in Briefs	Cheering Meerkats

Read the phrases.

Set 1	Set 2	Set 3
early one morning	animal welfare	fiendishly difficult
the earth's core	a careless mistake	a piece of chocolate cake
learn this story	a nightmarish journey	the diesel engine
have you heard	a hare-brained idea	he's so conceited
yearning for the holidays	barely a breath of wind	a deceitful child
lots of rehearsals	in the warehouse	the brilliant fielder
a good earner	comparing like with like	go and see my niece
pearly white	what a daredevil	don't sneer like that
do your research	not a care in the world	jeering is horrid
he overheard everything	a barefaced lie	he is a pioneer
a dearth of talent	he's a thief	what a mountaineer
an excellent researcher	the chief of police	he said cheerfully
don't stare	don't believe a word	an eerie noise
a rare bird	up to mischief	steer clear of that
prepare the dinner	a brief holiday	many volunteers
over the bare ground	take your receipt	veered from side to side
be aware of it	a long siege	a herd of reindeer
share these sweets	seeing is believing	they all cheered
very daring indeed	up on the ceiling	the sheer cliff
look at the scarecrow	unbelievably hard	they seem cheerier now
20 phrases	20 phrases	20 phrases

	up to 29 Sparking	30–39 Glowing	40–49 Burning	50–59 Sizzling	60+ Red hot!
Score/Date					
Score/Date					

23

ore

| or | au | aw | ore |

Carnivores Galore!

By Nic

Read the words.

Set 1 (11 words)	Set 2 (17 words)	Set 3 (17 words)	Set 4 (17 words)	Set 5 (17 words)
explore	therefore	forearm	footsore	omnivore
shore	spore	implore	eyesore	herbivore
snores	swore	restore	forehand	moreover
carnivores	ore	boredom	forewarn	forecaster
galore	bore	deplore	scorecard	imploring
sycamore	core	ashore	foreleg	foreboding
store	pore	encore	forearms	restoring
ignore	sore	forehead	offshore	deploring
before	tore	adore	forelock	adoring
more	wore	folklore	implored	exploring
gore	chore	forecast	restored	semaphore
11 words so far	score	adored	deplored	deplorable
	chores	foreseen	forewarned	adorable
	scores	foreground	explored	restorable
	pores	onshore	foresight	exploration
	explore	foretell	forebears	restoration
	seashore	bookstore	unexplored	restorative
	28 words so far	45 words so far	62 words so far	79 words so far

One Minute Wonders

	up to 39 Sparking	40–49 Glowing	50–59 Burning	60–69 Sizzling	70+ Red hot!
Score/Date					
Score/Date					

24

Read the story then draw the picture.

If you explore the shore beside the lake, you will hear some very loud snores! Carnivores galore are fast asleep under the sycamore tree next to their store of juicy meat. Tiptoe past and they might ignore you; make a noise and, before long, there might be more gore!

Practise writing.

Build your word power.

Brilliant! You made it to the next stage!

Two days on the bus from Perth to Adelaide, but you stop to swim with the sea lions and dolphins in Baird Bay, which you adore. It eases your sore legs and restores your energy levels. You start off the marathon feeling good. However, after 24 kilometres, you have a sharp pain in your hip and double up, hands on knees. You have to take it very easy after that and have an ice bath in the evening. You feel that a four-hour marathon is a respectable achievement at this stage.

Well done!
ear
ey
ore
eer
ie ei
are
ear
ch (k)
air
Silent Letters
y → i

ey

Monkey with the Money

By Lulu

| e | e-e | ee | ea | -y | ie | ei | ey |

Read the words.

Set 1 (10 words)	Set 2 (12 words)	Set 3 (12 words)	Set 4 (12 words)
monkey	keys	parley	hackney
donkey	trolley	keyhole	jockeys
journey	pulley	covey	whiskey
valley	alley	parsley	chutney
turkey	hockey	barley	Guernsey
chimney	volley	curtsey	chimneys
honey	galley	monkeys	spinney
abbey	medley	valleys	curtseying
key	kidney	journeys	volleying
money	motley	trolleys	volleyball
10 words so far	lackey	turkeys	alleyway
	jockey	donkeys	baloney
	22 words so far	34 words so far	46 words so far

	up to 39 Sparking	40–49 Glowing	50–59 Burning	60–69 Sizzling	70+ Red hot!
Score/Date					
Score/Date					

Read the story then draw the picture.

This is the tale of a monkey called Mike. With his good friend Donkey, he made the long journey to the far end of the mystical valley. There, he found a huge turkey sitting on a chimney eating golden honey. "Go to the old abbey with this magic key," squawked the turkey.

Behind a heavy wooden door, there were piles of coins. Now Mike is the monkey with the money!

Practise writing.

Build your word power.

Brilliant! You made it to the next stage!

Well done!
ear
ey
ore
eer
ie ei
are
ear
ch (k)
air
Silent Letters
y → i

The bus journey to Melbourne is eight hours. Your penultimate marathon needs you to have grit as it is the Midnight Marathon. You start at midnight and do 100 laps of an athletics track. You think of the force of five times your body weight slamming through each foot with every step. No wonder your ligaments and tendons become sore. Two blisters have returned, causing a sharp pain at each stride you take. You dream of honey sandwiches for breakfast at 4am!

ear

eer | ear

Read the words.

Set 1 (6 words)	Set 2 (20 words)	Set 3 (20 words)	Set 4 (20 words)
ears	**clear**	shearing	bleary
tears	**hear**	tearful	spearfish
year	**near**	earflaps	dogeared
fear	**ear**	hearing	eardrum
shears	**appear**	spearing	fearlessly
dear	gear	yearling	overhear
6 words so far	rear	clearance	appearing
	beard	spearmint	appearance
	spear	earache	endearing
	sear	earshot	tearfully
	smear	fearing	drearier
	smeared	gearbox	fearlessness
	speared	clearly	bleariest
	spears	hearings	disappear
	earful	nearing	ear-splitting
	nearby	yearly	disappeared
	dearly	endear	disappearing
	fearful	earrings	appearances
	appeared	fearless	overhearing
	weary	nearest	disappearances
	26 words so far	46 words so far	66 words so far

One Minute Wonders

	up to 39 Sparking	40–49 Glowing	50–59 Burning	60–69 Sizzling	70+ Red hot!
Score/Date					
Score/Date					

Read the limerick then draw the picture.

A koala with very big ears
Decided to never show tears
He lasted a year
Without any fear
Then along came a man with some shears.
Oh dear!

Practise writing.

Build your word power.

Brilliant! You've done it!

You are feeling weary but excited as you have nearly completed your challenge. Tasmanian Devil road signs appear on the way to the Cadbury Marathon start in Hobart; too many of these endearing creatures are killed on the road. Beginning outside the Cadbury factory, you push yourself to do your best time on this fast and flat course. Your legs are lead at the finish but you're elated with your time of 3 hours 25 minutes! You have done it!

Sizzling Syllables! ③

Read the syllables.

New *Run Australia* patterns

nore	ley	near	key	dore	gear
dear	core	ney	fore	fear	bey

Got it? ☐

Run Australia mix-up

chron	key	lair	bore	ceit	prie	ceil
fasten	rear	ware	fair	crumb	gnash	earl
chem	ney	neer	earth	mare	leer	ield
gore	bey	pare	hear	dair	plore	knock
fear	lore	sign	earn	ceive	teer	orch
autumn	tech	iece	doubt	lare	sear	hare
ley	fore	receipt	synch	fien	cheer	ney

Got it? ☐

WordBlaze so far

glor	dain	ack	brow	utch	ives	oof
ar	pare	weet	gyp	ceive	tion	oit
cise	oes	teer	low	kee	fore	traw
ture	guil	ream	flir	tur	pry	mea
whine	stru	ight	cray	ouch	cept	noy
gel	key	ceit	adge	mech	groa	shew
age	nue	ous	scoo	ock	cer	half
lieve	kin	ive	wreath	blear	otch	ress
ight	bair	fy	wa	oast	trum	wor
par	ule	ger	eck	ess	mar	oid

Got it? ☐

 30

Fiery Phrases! ③

Carnivores Galore!	Monkey with the Money	Big Ears

Read the phrases. Do you remember all the spelling patterns you have learnt so far?

Set 1	Set 2	Set 3
he scored two goals	a successful jockey	a fearless fighter
a very sore foot	play some volleyball	such painful earache
the weather forecast	in the galley	another appearance
so many chores	a motley crew	an ear-splitting crash
the offshore wind	cut the barley	he speared a fish
explore the caves	add some parsley	leave the keys
in the foreground	good at volleying	down the chimneys
two apple cores	hand over my money	the main torchbearer
go ashore now	how many turkeys	she sneered at him
a powerful forehand	at the start of the year	take my handkerchief
a game of hockey	nearing the end	he fielded well
up the narrow chimney	long, bushy beard	it's inconceivable
down in the valley	out of earshot	dare to be different
really delicious honey	he appeared again	a threadbare carpet
what a journey	dearly love to go	turn on the searchlights
look at the donkey	the nearest town	a quick learner
the monkey is eating	at the rear	play some chords
pull that heavy trolley	rather tearful	a beautiful schooner
in the dark alley	clearly seen again	time to drop anchor
look through the keyhole	what pretty earrings	a state of disrepair
20 phrases	20 phrases	20 phrases

	up to 29 Sparking	30–39 Glowing	40–49 Burning	50–59 Sizzling	60+ Red hot!
Score/Date					
Score/Date					

Blazing Extras

Read the words.

Bear with a Tear

By Ana

bear	swear	sportswear	tearaway
wear	swears	wearing	underwear
pear	footwear	bearer	tearable
tear	menswear	bearskin	pallbearer
bears	tearing	bearlike	forbearance
pears	antbear	overbear	unbearable
tears	forebears	wearable	unbearably
wears	outwear	bearable	overbearing

The Roaring Boar

By Madeline

board	hoary
oar	uproar
boar	hoarfrost
roar	keyboard
soar	outboard
hoard	snowboard
hoarse	cupboard
coarse	overboard

Unique Technique

By Jack

cheque	boutique	baroque
mosque	technique	opaque
clique	antique	oblique
plaque	physique	picturesque
unique	grotesque	statuesque

Door on the Moor

By Courtney

door	spoor
poor	moor
floor	boor

A Severe Sphere

By Ethan

here	severe	atmosphere
mere	cashmere	biosphere
sincere	adhere	persevere
interfere	merely	insincere
sincerely	revere	cereal
sphere	austere	coherent
sere	hemisphere	incoherent

Such Behaviour from a Neighbour!

By Ethan

favour	saviour
harbour	fervour
splendour	vigour
glamour	tumour
humour	succour
neighbour	tambour
rumour	behaviour
labour	endeavour
honour	enamour
journey	journalist
rigour	journalism

Year 5 and 6 words with no home!

twelfth

yacht

attached

programme

amateur

definite

develop

recommend

White Hot Wonder!

Read the words.

Set 1	Set 2	Set 3	Set 4
school	appear	earlier	fearlessness
early	happiness	tidiness	aching
armies	unearthed	receive	governments
thief	comb	kneading	daredevil
knock	restore	welfare	adorable
peer	chord	silkiest	airless
hairy	money	herbivore	alleyway
snore	priest	technology	architecture
learn	fairy	valleys	funnily
autumn	fearful	glistening	cheerfully
donkey	rustle	disappearing	research
dare	deer	volunteer	volleying
choir	chemical	enemies	doubtful
chore	nearby	rehearsal	jeering
beautiful	wheelchair	foreigner	repairing
jockey	honey	clearance	conceited
shrieking	forearm	prepared	searchlights
earned	easier	fairies	earlier
sign	briefest	chaos	protein
cheery	spies	yearning	unfairly
20 words	20 words	20 words	20 words

Beat your time!

Set 1	Set 2	Sets 1 and 2

Set 3	Set 4	Sets 3 and 4

34